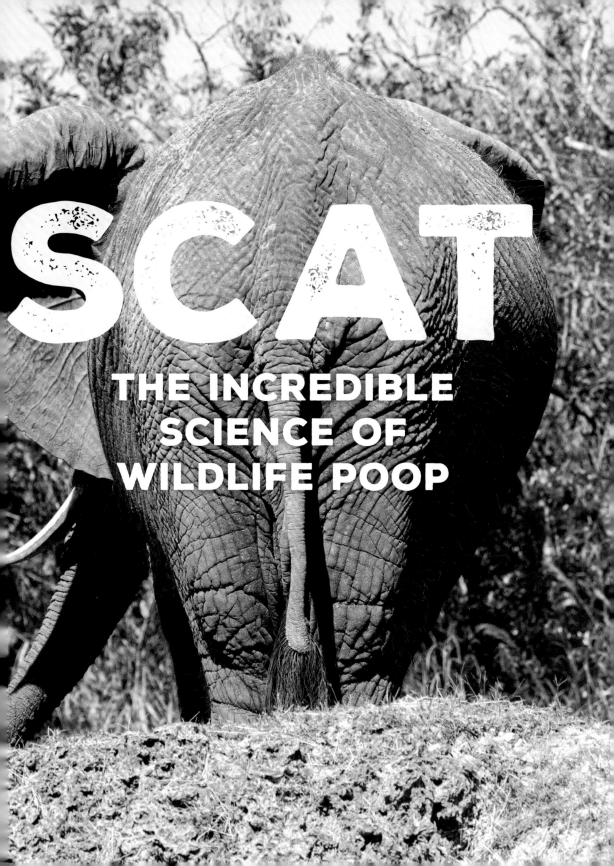

SCAT

THE INCREDIBLE SCIENCE OF WILDLIFE POOP

SCAT

THE INCREDIBLE SCIENCE OF WILDLIFE POOP

Featuring "A Field Guide to Scat in Your Neighborhood" by George Steele

Anita Sanchez

books for a better earth™

holiday house • new york

For you, future scientist, holding this book.

A Books for a Better Earth™ Title
The Books for a Better Earth™ collection is designed to inspire young people to become active, knowledgeable participants in caring for the planet they live on. Focusing on solutions to climate change challenges and human environmental impacts, the collection looks at how scientists, activists, and young leaders are working to safeguard Earth's future.

Library of Congress Cataloging-in-Publication Data

Names: Sanchez, Anita, 1956– author.
Title: Scat : the incredible science of wildlife poop / Anita Sanchez.
Description: First edition. | New York : Holiday House, [2025] | Series: Books for a better Earth | Includes bibliographical references and index. | Audience: Ages 8–12 | Audience: Grades 4–6 | Summary: "An introduction to the nutrient cycle and how scientists are using animal poop to study endangered animals, replant forests destroyed by wildfire, and more"—Provided by publisher.
Identifiers: LCCN 2024035460 | ISBN 9780823456185 (hardcover)
Subjects: LCSH: Animal droppings–Juvenile literature. Animals—Food—Juvenile literature. | Animal behavior—Juvenile literature.
Classification: LCC QL768 .S26 2025 | DDC 591.479—dc23/eng/20240810
LC record available at https://lccn.loc.gov/2024035460

ISBN: 978-0-8234-5618-5 (hardcover)

EU Authorized Representative: HackettFlynn Ltd, 36 Cloch Choirneal, Balrothery, Co. Dublin, K32 C942, Ireland. EU@walkerpublishinggroup.com

CONTENTS

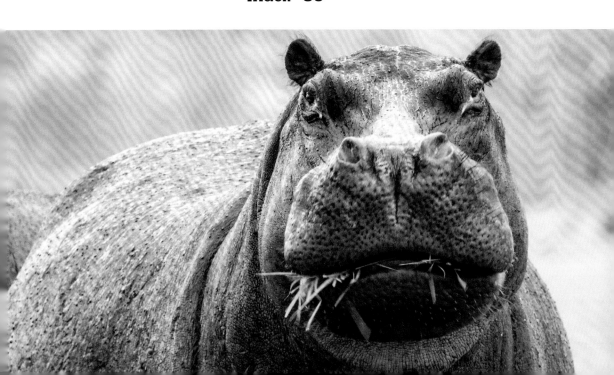

To find scat, you have to be in the right place at the right time.

CHAPTER 1:

The Science of Poop?
You've Got to Be Kidding!

Poop? Ugh! What could be more revolting, useless, and downright disgusting?

But in nature's endless and complex cycles, there's no such thing as waste. The poop of wild animals isn't just a big pile of pollution. Poop—or **scat**, as wildlife biologists call it—is full of surprising power. It can be food. It can be shelter. It can be life. And okay, it can be smelly.

The seeds that are sometimes carried in scat can create whole forests. Scat can be fertilizer for oceans and prairies. And scat is like a coded message that an animal leaves behind. Sometimes animals use it to "talk" to other members of their own species. But sometimes scat is talking to us.

For anyone who wants to learn about wildlife, scat is like a website filled with information. Humans can use scat to learn about animals—where they go, what they eat, and even what mood they're in. Scientists are struggling to find ways to help wildlife, and scat can reveal clues about how animals are responding to climate change threats like temperature changes, drought, and habitat loss.

Scat can give us a wealth of information about wildlife and their habitats.

JUST WHAT *IS* POOP, EXACTLY?

No matter if it's human or hippo, parrot or puppy, whale or worm—every animal's digestive system basically works the same way. It's a long tube where food goes in one end and waste comes out at the other.

SCAT SCIENCE: WAYS TO SAY POOP

We call it all sorts of things—doo-doo, poo, droppings, and other words you can't say in polite company. But scientists use the term *scat* to describe the excrement of wild animals, as opposed to human waste or farm animals' manure. The word **dung** usually refers to the big, moist splat of large **herbivores** (plant eaters) like cows or bison. The poop of insects, tiny as grains of pepper, is called **frass**. And the waste of flying creatures like birds and bats is called **guano**.

The food goes into the mouth and is chewed, mashed, or scrunched into tiny bits. Then, the mush is swallowed down into the gut, where powerful chemicals and bacteria attack it. The food is dissolved by stomach acids, chewed on by bacteria, and broken down into smaller and smaller specks until it's a slushy liquid. As the slush passes through, the body absorbs some of the good stuff—**nutrients**, vitamins, and minerals—soaking them up like a sponge. A lot of the water that was inside the food is soaked up too. Some of the useful stuff goes into the body—everything else comes out the other end.

IN ONE END, OUT THE OTHER

A bug's digestive tract might be half an inch long; a horse's is a hundred feet long. A whale's innards could be longer than a

In one end and out the other. This warthog plainly wasn't expecting to get caught on camera.

football field! Your intestines, if you spread them all out in a straight line, might be thirty feet long! Of course, no one is thirty feet tall—the intestines are all coiled up inside your body.

Ick! The stuff that comes out doesn't look like food anymore. Or does it? Sometimes there are bits that don't get digested. If the critter is a **carnivore** (meat eater), there might be leftover scraps of bones, fur, or feathers in the scat. If it's an herbivore, there might be bits of bark, stems, or seeds. (Remember this—it'll be important later on.)

Elephants spend most of their day eating, so they're constantly digesting and **excreting.**

SMELLY SIGNPOST

If you happened to be walking your dog along a trail and saw a pile of scat in the middle of your path, you'd hastily jump over it and go on your way. But your dog would want to sniff it, and sniff and sniff aaaand sniff some more. That's because to the sensitive nose of non-human animals, scat reveals a ton of information: what kind of animal has passed by, how long ago, what species.

An animal can't send a text, make a phone call, or put up a sign for another animal that might be miles away. But the animal can poop, and that's what it does. Often the pile is in an open, obvious space—the middle of a trail, a clearing in the woods, on top of a log—where someone else might bump into it hours or days later.

Scat scent can help a young

SCAT SCIENCE: WHY DOES PET POOP SMELL BAD BUT WILDLIFE SCAT DOESN'T?

Ugh! Your nose tells you that your dog has made a mistake indoors . . . or that it's time to clean the litter pan. No doubt about it, pet poo smells awful. But wild animals don't stink up the great outdoors in the same way. Wildlife scat is filled with odors, but they're mostly not the kind that human noses notice.

Wild animals eat food they find in the natural world, that their ancestors have been eating for millions of years. Pets, on the other hand, are fed a human-designed diet of things their stomachs didn't evolve to eat—corn, seaweed, potatoes, ground-up fish scraps. All kinds of odd bits and pieces go into commercial pet food. (If you don't believe me, read the ingredients on a bag of kibble sometime.) This artificial diet is often not well digested, so bits of it pass through the stomach and aren't broken down till they reach the end of the digestive system, called the colon or the large intestine. This process produces gases like methane and hydrogen sulfide, which result in smelly poop.

An elephant poops a lot—sometimes more than a dozen times a day.

animal find its mom or avoid predators. Or scat can send a strong message to rivals: *This is my territory—stay away.* An animal might use scat to announce that they're looking for a mate: *Hey, come on over this way!*

ARE YOU READY TO TAKE A CLOSER LOOK?

Poop or scat—whatever you want to call it—isn't the same thing as garbage. Scat has an unexpected but crucial part to play in nature. In fact, it's not too much to say that poop is powering our planet.

As it has for millions of years.

SCAT LOVERS: NAKED MOLE RATS: WE ALL SMELL GOOD!

The weird small mammals known as naked mole rats live in colonies underground, with tunnels and chambers dug out of the earth. They always have one room set aside as the bathroom, where everyone in the colony goes to poop. Every now and then, each mole rat ambles down to the bathroom and has a good roll in the poop pile. That way, all the rats in a colony smell the same. One sniff can tell a rat who's a friend and who isn't.

CHAPTER 2:

The Dance of Life: Plants and Animals Depending on Each Other

It's springtime in the forest—a forest of thirteen million years ago. A huge animal like an enormous, long-nosed bear lumbers through the trees. It's a giant ground sloth, one of the biggest mammals of the Cenozoic Era—as big as UPS truck and as tall as a giraffe.

This huge animal needs lots of food to keep his enormous body moving. He's an herbivore, so he reaches up to the trees, balancing on hind legs propped by a massive tail and pulling down branches with giant claws. He gobbles leaves, berries, and all sorts of fruits, but his favorite treat is wild avocados.

After stuffing in as many avocados as he can get his huge paws on, he wanders off in search of other snacks, moving slowly through the trees. And eventually, he does what every living thing does after a big meal. His body needs to get rid of the parts of the food it hasn't used, including the hard avocado pits. So he **excretes**.

And giant sloths could create a lot of poop—a big, steaming mountain of it. Giant sloth plops are definitely not something you'd want to step in. But this pile of scat wasn't garbage: it was a prehistoric garden. The dung pile was filled with avocado pits, which are the seeds of the plant. Where the giant sloths had passed, avocado seedlings sprang up behind them. Giant sloths were like big, furry farmers, planting groves of avocado trees.

So when you eat guacamole, you're eating the favorite food of the giant ground sloth. But have you seen any giant sloths lately?

Over the centuries, giant sloths became fewer in number—no one knows exactly why. Thousands of years ago, these huge animals became extinct. And this was an absolute disaster—from the point of view of the avocados.

THINKING LIKE AN AVOCADO

We've been looking at this from the animal's point of view—they need food, they eat plants for food. Works out great for the animals, right? But what if, for once, we looked at the world from the plants' point of view? What's in it for them?

Thousands of species of plants depend on animals to spread their seeds around. These plants couldn't exist without their animal farmers to do their planting for them. So plants advertise their wares to their seed-dispersing customers. Most fruits are tasty, sweet-smelling, or brightly colored so they stick out in the landscape, almost as though the plants are saying, *Come eat me!*

And the best part (from the plants' point of view) is that animals don't deposit their waste immediately after eating—it takes hours or even days for their bodies to digest a meal. By the time the waste is ready to be pooped out, the animal may have traveled many miles from the parent plant. The seeds spread to a whole new environment to grow. One plant can send thousands of its "babies" far and wide, encased in a coat of fur or feathers.

Plants don't have brains, of course. They didn't sit around thinking out this clever strategy. But over millions of years, plants and animals have evolved together. It's a win-win, although neither side is trying to help the other just to be nice. The plants take advantage of an efficient way to disperse seeds far and wide. The animals get a reliable source of tasty food. Plants benefit, and so do the animals—it's like a dance with two partners depending on each other to create something new.

When giant sloths went extinct, avocados could have followed them. Few other creatures were large enough to excrete the big seeds whole. Fortunately for the avocados, humans eventually took over the giant sloths' role. People discovered that avocados are nutritious and delicious and that if you put an avocado pit in the ground, it will grow into an avocado tree. To this day, people grow avocados on farms, carefully planting the seeds in orchards (by hand).

DOES A BEAR POOP IN THE FOREST?

Fast forward a few million years from the jungle of the giant sloths to a present-day forest in Rocky Mountain National Park. A sleepy bear lumbers through the forest. He's hungry and a little cranky after a long nap—so don't get in his way! But don't worry, he's not looking for people to eat. This bear is in the mood for a sweet treat.

He sniffs out the bushes where the fruit grows thickest: raspberries and blackberries and purple wild grapes. Reaching into the branches of a wild cherry tree, he pulls down his favorite treat: juicy red chokecherries.

Then, after a snooze, he does what the giant sloth did—what every living thing does after a meal. His body needs to get rid of the parts of the food it can't use, including the berry seeds and fruit pits. And black bears create a lot of poop—not as much as a

Each bear scat usually weighs more than a pound.

giant sloth, but still, quite a bit. More than enough to fill a Ziploc sandwich bag full.

A GREENHOUSE OF SCAT

Trish Stockton, a research biologist at Rocky Mountain National Park, always takes a few plastic sandwich bags with her when she walks the forest trails. She's hoping to be able to fill them—not with lunch, but with bear poop. She's thrilled when she finds one packed with seeds.

"I was pretty excited when I saw the volume of seed in the scat," she says, admiring her latest find. "To find a pile with that many seeds in it, I knew I was on my way." Trish has been trying to grow chokecherries and other native plants in the research greenhouses at the national park. But chokecherry seeds have a rock-hard coating, and it's almost impossible to get them to **germinate** (start to grow). Put them in a flowerpot, and they just sit there and slowly rot away. Chokecherries won't germinate until their tough outer shells have been **scarified**, or weakened somehow. To grow best, chokecherries must take a trip through a stomach.

The seeds are hard and bitter, so they don't get chewed—they just slip down the gullet into the stomach, where acids in the animal's digestive tract start to dissolve the hard shell. When the critter finally excretes the chokecherry seed, it's all ready to get growing.

And, as a bonus, the pooped-out seed is surrounded by a convenient mound of fertilizer. All the other soft, mushy stuff in the dropping contains minerals and nutrients the plant needs to grow strong. Scat is like a vitamin pill for plants.

A future forest!

Trish and other biologists had spent hundreds of hours gathering seeds and trying to get them to germinate with little success. Then she spotted the mound of bear scat. She planted bits of scat in the park greenhouse and waited to see what would happen.

One by one, tiny green shoots began to poke above the potting soil. Dozens of them, then hundreds! More than a thousand seedlings sprouted from the seeds contained in a single bear dropping.

Soon, the park's greenhouse was filled with thriving cherry saplings, grapevines, and berry bushes. "We've tried to grow these before and it took a lot of effort," biologist Kevin Gaalaas says. "This by far took a lot less effort and got more results than ever before. Sometimes, Mother Nature does a heck of a better job than we do."

The scat seedlings grew twice as tall as the human-grown sprouts. Next spring, Trish will go out and plant them all over the park, where they'll feed generations of hungry bears—and other animals too.

Scat disperses seeds over time as well as wide areas. Seeds don't have to germinate right away. They can lie dormant in the soil, as though they're asleep. Seeds can hang around for months, years, even centuries, waiting, waiting till the rains finally come and conditions are just right for germination.

It's the same story all over the world. Elephants poop out mango seeds and leave behind shady groves of mango trees. Chickadees eat berries and excrete the seeds to grow new forests. The slow digestive systems of Galápagos giant tortoises give them lots of time to disperse seeds far and wide as they lumber along.

CREATING THE LAND

Whether it's a giant sloth or a tiny mouse, every animal's scat

Sumac is just one of many common roadside plants that are natural bird feeders.

helps create the **ecosystem** it lives in. An ecosystem is a community of living things that interact with one another and with their environment. An ecosystem includes everything—every plant, animal, and bacteria, from the most ferocious predator to the smallest scrap of algae. An ecosystem also includes the non-living environment: sunlight, air, and soil. All these parts interact with and depend on one another.

Some animals are so important that their ecosystem couldn't exist without them. They play a critical role in keeping the ecosystem alive. These species are called ecosystem engineers.

Some of these ecosystem engineers change the landscape in obvious ways—for example, beavers creating wetlands where other animals live. Or prairie dogs that dig holes that create shelter. But many animals engineer their ecosystem one splat at a time.

No matter where you live, look around and think about it! Could your landscape have been created by the power of scat?

SCAT IN YOUR NEIGHBORHOOD: WHITEWASH ON THE WINDSHIELD

Ever park the family car under a tree and, in the morning, find streaks of white? If you happened to park beneath a tree that has tasty fruits, like mulberry, crab apples, or wild cherry, that might explain it. Birds flock to the tree, eat the fruits, and after their snack, they poop, which falls on whatever's below. They're not aiming at your car, even though it seems that way.

If you look at the white streaks with a magnifier, you might see tiny specks. Many fruits have small seeds that slip right through the tiny digestive tract of a songbird. When the bird flies away and poops in a new area, new trees are planted far from the mother tree.

CHAPTER 3:

Counting on Scat: An Information Dump for Wildlife Researchers

Tigers are in trouble. Once there were more than a hundred thousand tigers on the continent of Asia. But for centuries, they've been hunted for their beautiful fur coats. Today, it's illegal to hunt a tiger, but poachers still kill them for their skins or for other body parts, which are used in some traditional medicines. Tigers are also struggling with the loss of their rainforest habitat due to people logging the trees and clearing the land for houses or farms. We know their numbers have hugely declined, but no one knows exactly how many tigers are left. So wildlife biologists desperately need information about tigers in order to make conservation plans to save them.

But how do you find out how many tigers are living in a forest? It might seem as though it would be easy to spot a bright orange tiger in a green jungle. But you could walk through a dense Asian forest for weeks and never see one. Tigers are most active at night. They're very wary of humans. And they're really, really good at hiding. That gorgeous pattern of black stripes on orange fur actually helps them blend into patterns of shade and sunlight.

So how can you count tigers that don't want to be seen? How about paw prints? The track of an animal's foot in the mud can be helpful, but it's very hard to identify an individual from its print,

Tigers need our help to survive.

which isn't often clear enough to show clues that would help tell one tiger from another.

You could use cameras, set up throughout the habitat. But rain-forests are dense with leaves, and cameras only show what's right in front of them. Even the most sensitive motion-detection lenses rarely pick up the elusive cats.

But the one thing that tigers aren't secretive about is their pooping habits. Tigers tend to **defecate** in obvious places to let other tigers know their territory borders. *This hunting ground is mine! Keep out!*

Tiger scat looks just like what you'd find in your cat's litter box, only a lot bigger. Tigers even scratch around and partly bury their poops like house cats do. By counting the scats found in an area, researchers can estimate how many tigers there are.

Another thing researchers learn from studying tiger scat is where the tigers go each day as they hunt and look for mates. Mapping the locations where scat is found reveals what routes the tigers use repeatedly. This became crucial when the National Highways Authority of India wanted to expand a road between two forested areas into a four-lane highway. Data from tiger scat proved that the road crossed a major tiger travel route, so under-passes were built so tigers could cross the highway safely.

THE WISDOM OF THE SCAT

Just as scat can send messages to the noses of wild animals, so scientists can learn from scat—not by smelling it, but by examining it in a laboratory. Uma Ramakrishnan is an Indian scientist who's an expert on wildlife. She tracks tigers through the forest, but her main goal is to find tiger scat. "[It's] almost like gold to me," she says. To Uma, tiger poops are nuggets rich with information.

She and her colleagues collect samples of tiger scat from places like the Bandipur Tiger Reserve and National Park in the south of India. They spend weeks hiking along narrow paths that tigers often follow, covering hundreds of square miles. Each time they find a tiger dropping, they place it in a jar filled with alcohol to preserve it. Back in the laboratory, they examine the specimens to uncover a treasure trove of information.

Scat can reveal a huge amount about an animal's health without a veterinarian having to lay eyes on the creature. By examining the scat under a microscope, a scientist can see the bacteria that were in the animal's stomach and get a good idea of how healthy the animal is. Studying scat also reveals if the animal has parasites like worms in its digestive system. (Your vet does the same thing to check for parasites in your dog or cat.) It's also possible to determine if the animal is carrying the germs of a disease, and researchers have to be careful, as some wildlife diseases are transmissible to humans by touch or even by breathing dust from dried scat.

But the most amazing thing of all is that a scientist can figure

SCAT SCIENCE: WHAT IS DNA?

DNA is a molecule that carries information. It's stored inside every living thing on Earth. DNA is found in special parts of each cell called chromosomes. Under a powerful microscope, DNA looks sort of like a twisted ladder. Each rung of that ladder is made up of combinations of proteins, and the arrangement of the rungs is unique to each living thing.

So with just a tiny sample—it can be scat, or other things like bone, hair, or blood—a scientist can identify not only the species but the individual. DNA is also used to solve criminal cases because humans can be identified by their DNA too.

out exactly which individual animal pooped out a particular dropping. Scientists like Uma do that by studying the mysterious substance known as deoxyribonucleic acid, or DNA. As the scat passes through the animal's digestive system, cells from the creature's body become embedded in the scat. And the DNA that is found in each cell can identify the animal as surely as a fingerprint.

Using scat is not only good for wildlife biologists, it's great for the animals too. Scat studies are replacing other ways of tracking animals' movements. It used to be that wildlife biologists would attach a bright, easy-to-see tag to the animal's skin or place a GPS unit or some other sort of tracking device on the ear or tail, but this process is stressful and sometimes painful for the animal being studied. A small animal must be trapped, and a large animal, like a gorilla, moose, or giraffe, must be captured, usually by being shot with a dart gun containing a dose of tranquilizer to make the animal sleepy and easier to handle. But the animal can be harmed or even die if the dose of tranquilizer isn't just right.

Catching a wild animal can be pretty stressful for the scientist too—especially if the animal is a creature that might want to eat you for dinner. Capturing a wild tiger to tag or examine it could be a life-or-death struggle for all concerned.

Now, with the power of scat, we can learn a huge amount of information about an animal without having to touch it, dart it, grab it, cage it, trap it—or even lay eyes on it.

SCAT FROM THE SKY

Emperor penguins live in the bitter cold habitat of Antarctica. With temperatures that often drop lower than fifty below zero and hundred-mile-an-hour winds, it's super hard for ornithologists to study these majestic birds, which are the largest species of penguin. For many years, no one knew much about the emperors— how they survived polar winters, where they went to lay eggs, or even how many there were.

As climate change warms the planet, Antarctica is changing. Seawater is warming, which harms the cold-water fish and other aquatic life that penguins feed on. Ice and snow are melting much earlier in the year than they used to. Baby penguins who haven't yet grown their warm insulating feathers can fall though the thinning ice and drown. And there may be other impacts of climate change on the penguins that no one is noticing because they're so hard to study.

It's become very important to track the numbers of emperor penguins and find out how climate change is affecting them. Fortunately, penguins poop.

When it's nesting season, hundreds or even thousands of the birds gather to hatch their eggs, staying in the same area for many weeks. All that scat leaves a mark on the snow that can be seen for a long way—even from outer space! Ornithologists have used satellite technology to identify emperor penguin colonies from the guano stains left on the ice and snow. They discovered many colonies of these endangered birds that no one knew existed.

ZOO DOO

How can you tell if a leopard is happy? They don't smile like a person or wag their tail like a dog. The best way to check on a leopard's well-being is to check its poop.

Clouded leopards are some of the rarest cats in the world. They live in the cloud forests of southeast Asia.

Scat is a valuable source of information for zookeepers. Many captive animals in zoos are wary of humans, making them hard to catch or even approach without stressing them out. And it's difficult to tell how an animal is doing just by looking at it from many yards away. By studying special chemicals called **hormones** in the droppings of zoo animals, zookeepers can learn all sorts of things to assist them in caring for the animals.

One of the best things about zoos is that endangered species of animals can have babies in a safe environment to increase the population. The presence of fertility hormones in scat can tell zookeepers that a female animal is ready to breed and help them help her through the process of gestation (pregnancy) and birth. It shows all sorts of things animals just can't tell us—if a female elephant is about to have her baby or if a young panda is ready to mate. Hormone analysis can help ornithologists figure out why whooping cranes aren't laying eggs or when a pair of bald eagles will nest.

Stress hormones in scat show that an animal is feeling fear and tension. Perhaps the creature needs more privacy to hide from zoo visitors constantly staring at it. At the National Zoo in Washington, DC, zoo researchers tracked the level of stress hormones in the feces of clouded leopards. These animals are shy and solitary and needed more places in their shelter where they could hide and feel safe. It took many tests of stress levels and adding more and more shelter by raising walls and planting shrubs until the leopards had calmed down and were feeling secure.

SO MANY WAYS TO USE SCAT

Scat can show us how many animals are in a habitat, where they're going, what they're eating, how healthy they are, if they're breeding—even if they're scared, stressed, or relaxed. And since

SCAT SCIENCE:
COMMUNICATION CHEMICALS

Hormones are chemicals produced by an animal's body. They're part of the body's communication system, and they travel through the blood carrying messages to the organs and cells. The body releases special stress hormones when danger threatens, getting the animal ready to fight or flee. Different chemicals, called fertility hormones, flow through the body when the animal is ready to breed.

Elephant scat can send a clear message about the animal's health.

scat lasts a long time, especially in dry places like deserts, we can mine information from it even years after the animal has left it behind. As climate change heats up, it's becoming ever more urgent to gather all the information we can about wildlife so we can plan to help them survive our changing world.

There's another very important use for scat that you might not have thought of. Scat is not only filled with information, good for dispersing seeds, and great fertilizer, it can even be tasty.

Scat for dinner, anyone?

SCAT SCIENCE: DINOS DID IT TOO

Seems like there's no end to the things scat can tell us. For example, want to know how hard a Tyrannosaurus rex could bite? Just look at its scat.

Most dino scat decomposed long, long ago. But just like some dinosaur bones were fossilized, so was some of their poop. A piece of fossilized scat is called a **coprolite**.

As you can imagine, big dinosaurs made some big poops. The largest coprolite discovered so far is more than two feet long and six inches wide.

Dino scat may be seventy million years old, but it still has much to tell us. Paleontologists examining T. rex coprolites weren't surprised to discover bits of bones in the scat. But the amazing thing was how thoroughly the bones had been crushed and ground into fragments, some no bigger than a grain of sand! The analysis of the long-ago scat revealed the massive bite force of T. rex's powerful jaws.

CHAPTER 4:
A Disgusting Dessert

I'm sorry, but before we go any further, we're going to have to talk about one of the very ickiest, grossest things about scat—the fact that it can be good to eat.

Eating poop?? You'd think nothing could be worse. But actually, scat can be really good food. Really. Not for you and me, but for certain species of animals.

Scat isn't just waste materials that the animal's body doesn't need anymore. Every bit of scat has some leftover nutrition inside. It's like if you had a huge meal but you just couldn't eat it all. You wouldn't call the leftovers waste and throw them in the garbage. You'd save them to eat later.

Remember we said that when an animal digests its food, its body absorbs nutrients, vitamins, and minerals? Yes, the animal absorbs some of that good stuff—but not every single molecule of it.

This is especially true of herbivores—animals that eat plants. Plants are made of cells with walls of stringy fibers called cellulose. That makes for strong stems, tough branches, and leaves that can stand up to wind and rain. But these tough fibers make plants difficult foods to digest. No matter how much the animal chews, no matter how strong the stomach acids are, some of the nutrition isn't absorbed and comes out the back end. And that nu-

Summertime, and the living is easy.

trition won't go to waste. Something will eat it.

Poop eating has a scientific name—it's called **coprophagy**. And it's dessert for lots of different kinds of animals.

SMALL EATERS

Let's start with the little guys. Thousands of species of insects are **coprophages** (poop eaters), including flies, termites, and hundreds of kinds of beetles. There's a whole family of insects known as dung beetles because they just love dung. Some kinds of dung beetles eat nothing else but! Others will sometimes eat bits of plants as well. Some dung beetles are quite picky about what kind of scat

Dung beetles eat scat and sleep in it too.

they'll munch—they'll eat only the droppings of elephants. Some specialize in buffalo dung. Others will only snack on kangaroo scat.

Many of these poop-loving bugs use scat as a nice, moist, warm and cozy place to lay eggs. Then when the eggs hatch into larvae, the babies are surrounded by a source of food.

How do all these insects find scat? They don't have noses like we do, but they do have antennae that are supersensitive to scents. Sometimes they can find a fresh pile of scat seconds after it hits the ground.

THE SECRET HABITS OF BUTTERFLIES

Maybe it isn't too surprising that insects like flies and dung beetles like to eat scat. But butterflies? There's nothing more beautiful, more delicate and fragile than a butterfly. Surely these gorgeous creatures don't get down in the dirt and eat that disgusting stuff?

Well, I'm sorry, but yes. It turns out that butterflies love scat—the more slimy and disgusting, the better, as far as the butterfly is concerned.

Butterflies seek out damp piles of droppings, drawn to them as though to a garden of bright flowers. They crouch on top of the pile, slowly fanning their kaleidoscope wings. Then, as if they were feasting on nectar from a flower, they uncurl their long tongues and sip.

Butterflies love slime.

They need scat that's moist because they don't have the kind of mouth that can bite and chew. Instead, butterflies can only drink— they have a long tongue called a proboscis that uncoils and sucks up water and nutrients. They drink water from the scat, but it's more than just water they're looking for.

Usually we think of butterflies as sucking up flower nectar, but they need more than the sweet sugars of nectar. Scat is a restaurant for butterflies, with a handy drink as well as the minerals and nutrients the butterflies need for survival. They need certain salts and chemicals called amino acids, which are a kind of protein. And flowers just don't have enough of those chemicals.

So butterflies seek out things that do contain the salts and amino acids they crave. The very nutrients that butterflies need are found in things that come from an animal's body: poop, as well as blood, urine, and tears. (That's why you'll sometimes see photos of a flock of butterflies on the face of a crocodile or rhino: they're sipping moisture from the animal's eyeballs.)

PLANTS DO IT TOO

Ever hear of carnivorous plants (plants that eat animals), like the Venus flytrap? Botanists (scientists that study plants) have discovered there's a carnivorous plant that eats scat.

The toilet pitcher plant is shaped like a small, doll-sized toilet (I'm not making this up) with a bowl around four inches wide. It even has a lid that keeps rainwater out. The plant oozes a sweet, sticky nectar that attracts small rodents. Rodents poop very often, dozens of times a day, and as the little animal licks the plant's

A scat-eating plant.

sweet juice, it does its business in the tiny toilet. The plant then slowly absorbs the scat in a slow-motion flush.

BUT NOW THE REALLY GROSS PART

Okay, perhaps it's not too weird that bugs or even plants eat the scat of larger animals. But could there be any kind of creature that ... gulp ... eats its *own* droppings?

Yes indeed. Turns out a surprising number of animals do this.

SCAT LOVERS:
A HOME FOR FUNGUS

Some of the most enthusiastic lovers of scat aren't animals or plants—they're fungi. Unlike plants, fungi don't make their own food—they're like animals in that they have to find food. Thousands of species of mushrooms and other types of fungi live in or on top of animal droppings, sucking up the nutrition found in bison flops, coyote droppings, camel dung, panda poo, and countless other kinds of scat.

It's called **autocoprophagy**, and it's an important survival strategy for some mammals, especially during bitter cold winters.

Imagine a dark winter forest. Bare branches rattle in the icy wind. Every leaf is long since dead; every blade of grass is buried deep in snow. What is there for a hungry rabbit to eat?

In winter, cottontail rabbits don't hibernate like woodchucks or bears. They stay active, needing to seek out enough food to give their bodies energy to keep them warm every single day. They don't store up nuts or acorns like squirrels do, so there's nothing in the larder to eat on a cold morning. Except for scat.

In winter, rabbits feed on twigs, tree buds, and bark. This dry, tough, chewy diet is especially hard to digest. So after pooping, they go back for seconds. They nibble their own round droppings that look (but don't taste) a lot like Cocoa Puffs. It's how these animals extract every last bit of nutrition from their sparse meals of bark and twigs. The extra boost of nutrition helps to get them through the winter.

Wintertime, and the larder is bare.

SCAT SCIENCE: THE NUTRIENT CYCLE

The nutrients found in scat are ones that are needed by almost all living things. Scat contains nitrogen, potassium, phosphorus, calcium, and carbon, along with other elements. A rabbit, a butterfly, an oak tree, or humans like you and me—we all need those nutrients to survive.

Let's follow a single one of those nutrients: an atom of calcium, for example, found in an acorn. One chilly day in autumn, a hungry mouse nibbles on the acorn. The calcium goes into the mouse's stomach, is absorbed into its body, and becomes part of a leg bone.

But soon a hawk swoops down and carries off the mouse. Flying to an oak tree a hundred yards away, the hawk eats the mouse. The atom of calcium travels through the hawk's stomach and is excreted out in its droppings, which fall to the ground below the tree.

And guess what? The tree's roots suck up the calcium, and the molecule ends up in a twig . . . which is eaten by a rabbit, and nature's cycle starts again.

SCAT IN YOUR NEIGHBORHOOD:
TOO MUCH IS BAD

Too much animal waste all piled up in the same place can cause problems. Canada geese often gather by the hundreds at ponds in small town parks. Sometimes they're just stopping for a quick rest-and-snack break on their fall migration. But sometimes the geese stick around if it's a mild winter or if people feed them. And all that concentrated poop isn't healthy for the pond.

Just one goose can poop a quart of sticky, greenish guano every day. And too much of this nutrient-rich stuff fertilizes plants that grow in the pond. This can lead to a huge overgrowth of slimy algae. The thick green slime can fill a shallow pond, making it impossible for frogs, turtles, or salamanders to live there. And when the algae rots, the process of decomposition removes oxygen from the water. If too much scat accumulates, the pond may end up as a barren puddle with no life in it.

Even in tropical climates, where it's warm and sunny, some animals will eat their own poop. Whether you live in the rainforest or on the frozen tundra, meals of twigs, bark, and leaves are hard to digest. Inevitably, a lot of nutrition goes out the back end. Gorillas are one of the rainforest herbivores that scoop their own poop for food.

One of the many ways in which gorillas are like humans is they go *Mmmmmm* when eating something really tasty. Gorillas will poop into their hands and then eat their own scat warm, apparently enjoying each bite.

This seems the ultimate level of gross to us humans. But really, it's the ultimate level of recycling. Autocoprophages are using every last scrap of nutrition so that nothing goes to waste in the struggle for survival.

CHAPTER 5:

How to Grow a Whale

What weighs as much as twenty-five elephants, can hold its breath for an hour, and creates scat that is bright pink? Hint: it's the biggest animal on our planet.

The blue whale is the biggest whale there is, and these giants feed on some of the littlest things in the ocean. The scat these enormous whales produce is some of the most important scat in the world.

Blue whales are so incredibly big, it's hard to imagine. They're dinosaur big, three times longer than a school bus, with a heart the size of a small car. So you might think these giants are the Tyrannosaurus rexes of the sea, fierce predators with huge teeth. But actually, blue whales have no teeth at all. When a blue whale is hungry, it just opens its mouth, and the food goes in.

A hungry blue whale dives deep in the ocean. Far below the surface, the whale hunts for **krill**. These are tiny shrimplike creatures, each one about half the size of your pinky. They float in the ocean in huge masses, trillions of them forming dense clouds in the water. Their bodies have a shell-like covering that's colored dark pink, and their huge swarms turn the sea a reddish color. Krill sink deep into the ocean to breed and lay their eggs, and the whale swims after them.

The whale lunges into the mass of krill with mouth open wide. After inhaling a monster mouthful of food, the whale closes its jaws.

A blue whale's digestive tract can be more than seven hundred feet long. (That's longer than the Washington Monument.)

Long strips of filters in the whale's mouth, called baleen, strain out food particles, which then go down the throat whole—no chewing. This method of eating is called filter feeding.

You can imagine that it takes a lot of those little teeny krill to fill up a ginormous whale's stomach even for one day. A single krill weighs about .04 ounces. A blue whale can weigh in at three hundred thousand pounds. But what do all those krill find to live on in the deep, remote parts of the ocean?

Krill live by eating **phytoplankton**, which are microscopic plants so tiny that a million of them could literally fit in a teaspoon. They float in the seawater, and krill swarm up to them at night to feed. Without the phytoplankton, there would be no krill.

Like all living things, phytoplankton need nutrition to grow. But seawater isn't the likeliest place for plants to grow, you'd think. The soil of a garden is rich with nutrients. Seawater has water, yes, but not much else that living things need. All those trillions of little green specks can't grow without a healthy blast of fertilizer.

So how does the good stuff get to the phytoplankton? It's delivered right to them—literally pooped out on top of them.

PINK FERTILIZER

Farmers have known this dirty little secret for thousands of years: if you want your crops to grow well, poop on them.

Humans have long fertilized their crops and gardens by using the droppings of livestock (animals that are taken care of by people). Cow manure, chicken poo, rabbit pellets—no matter what kind of animals the farmer raises, manure is money in the bank.

Each tiny krill is a giant link in the food chain.

It's packed with the exact nutrients—nitrogen, calcium, phosphorus, potassium, magnesium, iron, and more—that plants can't live without.

A blue whale can take in more food in one gulp than any other creature. They eat between ten and twenty tons of krill in a day. Matthew Savoca is a researcher at Stanford University in California, and he's been studying what whales eat each day. "That amount of food is somewhere in the range of twenty to fifty million calories," he says. "That is about seventy to eighty thousand Big Macs. Probably decades of our eating is one day for them. So it's pretty remarkable."

All that supersize eating leads to a lot of scat. Each time a blue whale does its business, it gives off about fifty gallons of crumbly,

Whales do a headstand and then power a deep dive with their muscular tails.

watery scat. And like all scat, whale poo is filled with nutrients. It's especially high in iron, which phytoplankton need to fuel their fast rate of growth. Blue whale scat is colored pink because of the krill's pink shells.

Why is whale poop so important? Surely other things in the sea are going around pooping and could fertilize the phytoplankton? The reason is that whales dive deep to catch their food but must return to the surface to breathe. Whales are mammals, just like us, so they can dive while holding their breath (and they can hold it for a long time!), but sooner or later they have to come back to the surface to get air. That's when they poop. So they bring nutrients up from the deep and excrete on the surface, moving nutrients around in a never-ending cycle.

IT'S NOT JUST WHALES

Fish do it too, of course. Imagine all the trillions of fish in the sea. No matter if it's a five-hundred-pound tuna or a sardine as big as your finger, every fish in the sea has to poop. Fish poop is usually a jet of liquid waste, but it can also be in tiny pellets. But no matter what form it takes, fishy poo returns a blast of nutrition to the water that plankton and other seaweed can use for fertilizer.

Some fish hang around the same area all their lives, but many species of fish are wanderers, often traveling hundreds or even thousands of miles. Whale sharks, for example, go on long migrations of ten thousand miles or more. So when a fish eats in one place and then travels miles before it poops, the nutrients are being spread throughout the ocean.

And so it goes, with molecules of essential nutrients in constant motion. All the watery parts of the world are like a giant blender where the nutrients are constantly being stirred up and carried to new places. Scat is nature's tool for spreading the good stuff around. Without it, the ocean would be a wet, watery desert.

That's the good news. But the bad news is that there aren't as many creatures in the ocean as there used to be. Whales have been relentlessly hunted for centuries by humans who want to use them for food or for the oil that can be extracted from their bodies. In the twentieth century, whale hunters got so efficient that huge numbers of whales were killed. Blue whales are an endangered species, with only a fraction of their original population left. Almost all species of fish and marine mammals are declining in numbers due to a lot of reasons: pollution, overfishing, and, increasingly, climate change.

WARMING WATERS

One of the direst problems facing sea life is that the oceans of the world are changing. Human-caused air pollution puts carbon

SCAT IN YOUR NEIGHBORHOOD: A SHORT-LIVED GOLDFISH

Ever have a goldfish that mysteriously died? If the fishbowl is small and has too many fish, they can be harmed by their own scat. Goldfish scat is almost invisible, but too much of it pollutes the water and is toxic to the fish.

One way to solve this problem is to add plants. Plants in the aquarium water will act as natural filters, absorbing the scat and using it as fertilizer.

Dolphins can travel eighty miles in a single day.

dioxide and other gases into the atmosphere. These gases, called greenhouse gases, trap the sun's heat close to Earth and make global temperatures rise. The effects of climate change are felt in the sea as well as on land.

Warming waters are making it harder for plankton to grow. And it turns out that whales aren't the only creatures who need phytoplankton. We do too.

Phytoplankton make their food in the process known as photosynthesis. During this process, they give off oxygen. Scientists estimate that approximately half of the air we breathe is created by these little green specks.

Let me say that again—*half* of the air we breathe.

Phytoplankton also remove carbon dioxide from the atmosphere, helping to lower the amount of greenhouse gases. So if there are only a fraction of the whales left, that's only a fraction of the fertilizer going to the life-sustaining, oxygen-producing, climate-change-fighting phytoplankton.

For many years, we've known that whale numbers were getting lower and lower. Most countries ban the killing of whales, but poachers still hunt them. And many whales are killed by being hit by boats or tangled in fishing gear. All over the world, people have been working desperately to protect whales and their habitats, especially places where the whales go to feed and have babies.

But really, *why* is it so important to help the whales out? Unlike fish, whales aren't an important nutrition source for humans—only a few people actually use whales for food. Most people want to save whales just because they're so big, beautiful, and awesome.

But now it turns out that there's another reason to save the whales. Every single person on this planet needs the whales to keep the nutrient cycle rolling and protect the phytoplankton. Those little green specks can lower the effects of climate change—and help to keep us breathing.

Let's head back to dry land to meet another creature that fertilizes their own food. Or at least they used to, not too long ago.

SCAT LOVERS: PENGUINS IN THE POOP

When you think of penguins, you think of ice and snow, right? Some species of penguins raise their young on the snow, but one type of penguin, called the Humboldt penguin, has its babies in a big pile of scat.

The birds live along the coast of South America, and the land is too bare and rocky for the penguins to dig a burrow. But fortunately, there's scat! Seabirds have lived there for so many centuries that there's a layer of guano many feet deep. The penguins burrow into the soft guano to lay their eggs and raise their young.

But Humboldt penguin populations are getting smaller because they are losing their habitat. For years, people have mined the guano like gold—in fact, it's sometimes called "white gold." It's used as rich fertilizer for farm crops.

Baby Humboldt penguins need shelter from cold and rain and also from overheating in the sun. There were once hundreds of thousands of Humboldt penguins, but there are now only about twenty-four thousand. Ornithologists are working to create roofed shelters where the penguins can lay their eggs. The secure roof helps keep away rain, sun, and predators such as gulls.

CHAPTER 6:

SNOWDRIFTS OF SCAT: THE STORY OF THE PASSENGER PIGEON

The noise is faint at first—like a rumble of thunder, far away. There's a big black cloud in the distance—but it's moving faster than a cloud. The wind of its coming makes leaves rustle, branches bend. Then comes the roaring thundercloud, but it isn't a cloud, it's a flock of birds—hundreds, thousands, millions of birds! When they fly overhead, the day grows so dark that it seems like nightfall.

The immense flocks of the birds called passenger pigeons were incredibly huge. One flock was estimated to be a mile wide and three hundred miles long. It took days to pass overhead.

Simon Pokagon, a member of the Pokagon Band of Potawatomi, wrote about standing in awe to watch the birds on a bright spring day in 1850: "I have seen them fly in unbroken lines from the horizon, one line succeeding another from morning until night . . . I have seen them move in one unbroken column for hours across the sky, like some great river." He remembered how the feathered river would flow down over a valley and "pour its living mass headlong down hundreds of feet, sounding as though a whirlwind was abroad in the land." It was a sight he never forgot.

But this living waterfall of birds is a scene that no one now alive can remember. Passenger pigeons became extinct in 1914.

These incredible birds once lived in the eastern part of North America. Ornithologists estimate that there were three to five

The passenger pigeon—a bird we'll never get to see.

billion of them. They traveled around a lot (which is why they were called passenger pigeons), the huge flocks flying across the land, moving from forest to forest. Millions of pigeons would settle on the branches, almost more birds than there were leaves on the tree. Each bird only weighed a few ounces, but there were so many that thick branches would splinter under their weight. The pigeons would feed on acorns, beechnuts, chestnuts, seeds, and berries, clambering over the branches until they'd eaten all they could find. Then they were off again, rising into the air with a deafening roar as millions of wings beat the air.

And you can imagine, this amazing number of pigeons created an amazing amount of scat. A single pigeon poop is a small whitish splat, about a teaspoon of poop, which the bird squirts out several times a day. Multiply that by a billion or so. Eyewitnesses reported that after passenger pigeons had passed overhead, their scat lay across the land in white drifts like snow. In places where the pigeons hung out for a while, like their nesting sites, the scat was piled up two feet deep.

PIGEONS TODAY

Let's talk about pigeons. Not passenger pigeons, but a related species, the kind that hangs out in city parks today. You've seen them, strutting along with their soft, musical *coo coo roo coo*. They mingle boldly with people on the sidewalks, trotting along on pink feet, hardly seeming to notice the crowds until someone scatters a handful of breadcrumbs. Then they descend in a flock with wings clapping softly as they land.

Urban pigeons hang out on city streets.

Many people don't like pigeons because of all the poop they leave behind. And it's true, pigeon poops are large, sticky, and unsightly. The problem, as we've seen before, is that too much poop in one place is bad. Pigeons all concentrated in a park, hanging out because people feed them, is a problem. Whether it's too many geese at a pond, too many fish in an aquarium, or too many cows all crammed together in a pen, when poop is concentrated, nature doesn't have a chance to break it down and turn it into useful fertilizer.

So it might seem that the passenger pigeon blizzard of scat was a bad thing that would destroy the forests they fed on. But quite the opposite was true.

The forests that the passenger pigeons knew were different than the forests of today. There were trees tall as church spires, a hundred feet high. Some oak trees were as big around as a ring of ten people holding hands. Some trees were so big that farmers could stable their horses inside the hollow trunks.

When the pigeons broke branches of the huge old trees they landed on, it seems as though that would have been unfortunate. Hurting a branch certainly harms a tree. But it turns out there's more to it than that. Breaking the thick, leafy branches from the tops of the great trees allowed sunlight to pour all the way down to the forest floor. That's where the baby trees were struggling to grow in the deep shade. Lots of sunlight let the oak and beech seedlings get a healthy start.

And the soil these baby trees were growing in was fertilized by all that pigeon scat. Just like the whales, pigeons ate and then traveled before they excreted. So they carried nutrients over many

Oaks depended on the passenger pigeons as much as pigeons depended on the oaks.

miles, from one forest to another. Centuries of pigeon guano piling up created incredibly rich soil. The feast of nutrients in the pigeons' poo helped the trees grow to immense sizes, creating magnificent forests. And the well-nourished trees were able to produce huge crops of food: acorns, chestnuts, walnuts, beechnuts. These nuts, packed with protein, fed all kinds of animals as well as the pigeons: squirrels, deer, raccoons, woodpeckers, opossums, wild turkeys—and humans.

The Indigenous people that lived in the realm of the passenger pigeon watched for the coming of the huge nesting flocks in spring. After a long, hard winter, they would hunt the birds for a rich source of food. A pigeon stew or a roasted squab (young pigeon) was a nutritious meal filled with protein, and delicious too.

But the Native Americans also understood that the pigeons were beings worthy of respect. Some tribes had dances or ceremonies honoring the birds. To this day, members of the Haudenosaunee Confederacy perform the pigeon dance in remembrance of the passenger pigeon that nourished their ancestors.

They also knew that it was important to take care of such a great source of food. Many tribes had strict rules against killing adult birds that were nesting to ensure there would be parents to care for the young. Other tribes only hunted the birds at certain times of year or in preparation for special feasts.

Three hundred years ago, when the first ships arrived with Europeans coming to the New World, things began to change. The newcomers were awed at the vast flocks of birds and the huge trees they fed on. And unfortunately for the birds, the invaders soon discovered that they tasted really good.

There were so many passenger pigeons that it seemed as though they would never run out. And the pigeons were ridiculously easy to hunt. Just waving a long pole amid a low-flying flock would knock birds out of the air. Shaking branches would tumble the babies out of the nests by the thousand. At first, hunters only took what they needed to feed their families. But in the mid-1800s, passenger pigeons became big business. Professional hunters began killing and marketing huge numbers of them. Hunters would go to the birds' nesting grounds and slaughter them by the tens of thousands. The birds were shot, netted, poisoned, and trapped.

At the same time, the forest that the birds depended on for food and nesting sites were disappearing. Trillions of trees were cut down for lumber, papermaking, and firewood. The land was cleared to make room for farms and houses.

In the space of a few decades, almost all the pigeons were gone.

Pigeon hunts were a popular sport.

But still, no one took any action. One by one, the last few pigeons were shot and eaten for food. Finally, ornithologists desperately tried to breed the birds in a zoo. But it was too late. The last passenger pigeon died in a zoo in 1914. Of all those billions of birds, not a single one remained.

The passenger pigeons are gone now, gone forever. We'll never get to see that river of birds flying overhead and darkening the sky; we'll never hear the thunder of their wings.

But the passenger pigeons did us one last favor as they faded away forever—they gave us a wake-up call.

Mighty oaks, towering chestnut trees, eagles, salmon, beavers, moose, bison . . . for centuries, there was apparently no end to the riches of nature in North America. And so there were no laws protecting wildlife—anything was, literally, fair game. If a hawk was threatening your chickens, well, just shoot the hawk out of the sky. Want a snowy egret's plume to decorate your hat? Go right ahead. Birds stealing your grain? Just eliminate the birds. Why not? Plenty more where they came from.

But the shocking loss of the passenger pigeons proved that idea wrong. People began to pass laws to protect wildlife and even some of their habitats. Animals that had been pushed to the verge of extinction, like beavers, wolves, white-tailed deer, wild turkeys, and bison, began to make a slow but steady comeback. Today, endangered species are guarded by strict laws in most nations around the world. Animals that are abundant enough to be hunted usually have laws limiting the number that can be killed.

But perhaps we can learn another lesson from the sad story of the passenger pigeons. Too late, people realized that pigeons were

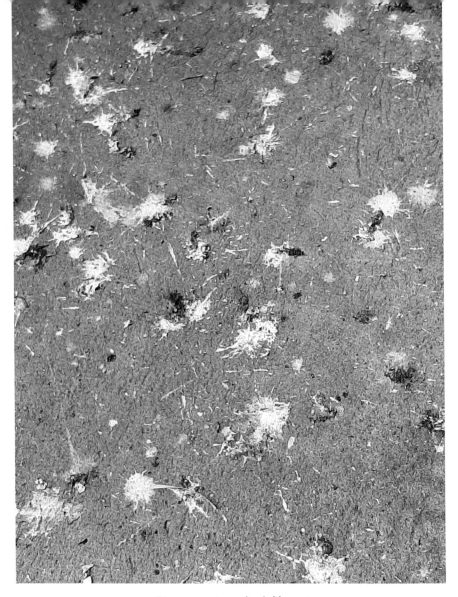

Pigeon scat can look like art.

an essential part of the forests the birds fed on. Like the whales, pigeons fertilized their own habitat, and in doing so, maintained the balance of life in their ecosystem. That benefited countless other species, including humans.

Are there other animals out there doing the same? What other ecosystem engineers are out there, busily pooping out the scat that can nourish whole ecosystems?

SCAT LOVERS: HIDING
IN PLAIN SIGHT

If you took a look at a greenish-white blob of bird scat sitting on a leaf, you might be surprised if it suddenly flew away. A type of North American moth, called the wood nymph, has beautiful patterns of green, white, and black on its wings. They look lovely in flight, but once they come to rest and fold up their colorful wings, they look exactly like a bird's dropping. It's a great way to outsmart predators.

Beautiful wood nymph, *Eudryas grata*, adult.

Beautiful wood nymph, *Eudryas grata*, folded.

CHAPTER 7:
Don't Forget to Flush!

The slow-flowing waters of the Mara River in Kenya, East Africa, are murky and green in the hot noonday sun. There are dozens of what look like big gray rocks in the quiet water. But as the sun goes down, the still water begins to ripple and churn, and then, slowly, a huge head rises to the surface. A giant mouth splits into a big toothy yawn. Then another head pops up, and another. Nighttime is when the hippos wake up!

One by one, the big animals heave themselves out of the water and clamber onto the riverbank. They slog slowly through the mud, plowing channels through the soft, wet earth. When they reach a grassy meadow, they start munching, tearing the plants with hard, bony lips and chewing the tough grass blades with huge teeth. They feast in the cool night air, each hippo packing away a hundred pounds or so of food.

Then, when the morning sun peeks over the horizon, they head back to the water. Hippos have skin that's sensitive to sunburn, so they can't linger in the sun for long. Even worse, their big bodies have no sweat glands, so they can't sweat to cool off like we do. Hippos on land risk getting dehydrated and can even die if they overheat. By the time the sun comes up, they're safely back in the cool river.

And after a big all-night meal, you know what happens, right? Yes.

Each time a hippo poops, it jets out gallons of watery green

Time for the hippos to wake up!

mush. You definitely wouldn't want to go swimming in a river where hippos hang out. (Also, the grumpy hippos would probably chew you up like a grass blade if you got too close.) To make matters worse, while hippos are pooping, they often whir their short tails around like a pinwheel, flinging slimy scat far and wide. (Another good reason not to get too close to a hippo.)

Hippos are enormous animals—a female hippo literally weighs a ton, and an adult male can weigh four tons or more. Biologists

Hippos eat, eat, eat all night long.

who have been studying this colony of hippos estimate that they dump eighteen thousand pounds of poop into the Mara River— every single day.

How disgusting is that?! Doesn't all that hippo poop pollute the river and harm other animals? A team of aquatic biologists who were investigating the Mara's water quality began to sniff out some of the bad effects of hippo scat.

WHAT'S THAT SMELL?

On a hot summer day in 2018, on the banks of the Mara River, something smelled bad. Rotten, disgusting, and really, really bad.

But the unpleasant smell wasn't caused by the hippos. All along the riverbank were thousands of dead fish. Fish bodies were piled up on the mud and floating in the green water.

Biologists investigating the cause of the fish kills took samples of water throughout the river. They found that the water in the shallow pools where dozens of hippos gather was super low in oxygen. As we've seen before, too much scat can be a problem. Large amounts of scat act like an overdose of fertilizer, causing a huge growth of algae. Then, when the algae dies, the process of decomposition sucks up oxygen from the water. Because of all the hippo dung, the oxygen in the river had dropped to very low levels, and the fish had suffocated.

So the answer to preventing fish kills seemed clear—get those hippos out of the river!

But wait. It's not like the hippos just arrived, waded into the river, and started messing things up. Hippos have been a part of the river ecosystem for quite a while. In fact, hippos were pooping in African rivers seven million years ago. The problem lies not with the hippos but with our changing planet.

Climate change is causing low levels of rainfall in some areas of the world, including many parts of Africa. Usually, the waste the hippos create is flushed downstream every day, in small amounts that the fish can handle. But if a drought causes water levels in the river to get too low, the poop can't wash away from the shallow pools. Like a stopped-up toilet, the waste builds up and up and up. Then, when the rains finally come, a big surge of water flushes deadly amounts of hippo scat downstream. As climate change means more areas in Africa are experiencing droughts, nutrient flushes are becoming an increasing problem.

FEEDING ON THE FLUSH

So, again, wouldn't it be great to get rid of the hippos and clean up the water?

Not so fast. Like all scat, hippos' icky, watery blasts are packed with powerful nutrients that plants and animals need. Hippo dung is filled with nitrogen, carbon, and phosphorus. And it's especially loaded with one really important nutrient: silica.

Silica is a mineral that is very hard—it's found as part of sand and rocks. Plants use molecules of silica to create their cell walls, building strong stems and leaves. The tough-leaved grass the hippos eat has lots of silica in it, so hippo poop is especially rich in this mineral.

Other grass eaters, like antelopes and zebras, have silica in their poops too. But their scat falls on the land, where it's sucked up by grass roots in a continuous cycle. Hippos do almost all of their pooing in the water, dozing all day in the cool of their shallow pools.

So hippos are especially important as ecosystem engineers because they do what no other animal in that environment is doing: carry nutrients from the land to the river. They're like a delivery truck endlessly going back and forth, eating here, pooping there, delivering nutrients that couldn't get to the water any other way.

Diatoms are tiny, but their impact on the river is huge.

And just like the blue whales fertilizing the phytoplankton in the sea, hippos fertilize tiny specks of algae floating in the river. Much of the plant life in African rivers is made up of a weird form of algae called **diatoms**. They're tiny, one-celled organisms, and they float in the river water in huge numbers, forming dense clouds that turn the water green. Each individual diatom is surrounded by a strong cell wall, which is made up almost completely of tough silica. So the diatoms can't exist without frequent deliveries of silica-filled hippo poop to their habitat.

And these tiny diatoms are the basis of almost every food chain in the river. They're especially important for the fish that swim in the murky water. And countless creatures depend on the river's fish for food. Long-legged water birds like herons, cranes, storks, and ibises hunt for fish in shallow pools, while kingfishers and pelicans scoop up fish from the deeper water. Reptiles like crocodiles and turtles hunt for fish, and along the banks, river otters dive to catch fishy prey. And it's not just wildlife—the people who live in the Mara valley also depend on fish as a major source of food. But the entire ecosystem depends on the diatoms—which depend on the hippos.

So it turns out that the whole food web of many African rivers is created by hippos and their scat. Get rid of all that gross hippo poop—and the entire ecosystem collapses.

But hippo numbers are declining as wetlands are drained to make way for towns, roads, and farmland. Many hippos are hunted by poachers who value the big animals for their meat and for their enormous ivory teeth, which are used in carvings and artworks. Droughts caused by climate change are affecting hippos too—they can't live without the water that cools them down from temperatures that are growing ever hotter.

HELPING HIPPOS

How to help the hippos help the river? The biggest need for these animals is enough space. Too many hippos crowded into a shrinking habitat means many more flushes of too much poop swirling downstream. Hippos need room to spread out—and that means wild rivers to roam in. Governments of many African nations and not-for-profit wildlife organizations are trying to preserve river habitats in the huge continent of Africa. The Mara River is hundreds of miles long and flows through several countries. Fortu-

Too many hippos or not enough river?

nately, many miles of it pass through the Masai Mara Reserve in
Kenya and the Serengeti National Park in Tanzania, where the
river is protected from development and the wildlife is guarded by
park rangers. Thousands of people from all over the world come
to marvel at the amazing diversity of animal life in and along the
river.

The hippos need the river to survive—just as much as the river
needs the hippos.

SCAT IN YOUR NEIGHBORHOOD: WORMS TO THE RESCUE

You probably don't have a herd of hippos fertilizing your backyard. But you do have a whole lot of earthworms burrowing around under the grass. And what hippos do for the rivers of Africa, earthworms do for your backyard.

Earthworms eat bits of leaves and grasses they find in the ground and poop it out. Worm poops, called castings, are tiny specks, nothing like the big splats of hippo dung. But we're talking about a million earthworms that can live in one acre of soil—those castings really add up.

As they eat their way through the soil, pooping as they go, they carry minerals from lower levels to higher, much like the fish and whales swimming through the sea. Nutrients like phosphorus, potassium, and calcium are carried from underground to the surface.

As earthworms move into a damaged, eroded area, their poop will fertilize it so that new grass can grow. Whether it's a worn-out farm field, an abandoned coal mine, or a small corner of your yard, worms can help heal damaged soil. They tunnel through compacted dirt, letting air and water in and fertilizing seeds. As plants grow, their leaves provide more worm food, so more earthworms can move in.

CHAPTER 8:

How to Heal the Earth

The fire had left the forest in ruins. The emerald-green rainforest had stood for centuries in the mountains of southern Mexico, but a wildfire had burned it to the ground. All the wildlife that once lived there had fled or been destroyed: birds, fruit bats, howler monkeys, jaguars, anteaters, butterflies, toads, and many more species. Charred stumps of trees dotted the blackened landscape.

All over the world, this is becoming a sad, familiar sight. As climate change creates droughts, forests dry out. Dead leaves and twigs pile up on the ground. Then a carelessly dropped match, or an untended campfire, or a lightning strike can become a roaring runaway wildfire that's almost impossible to extinguish.

A team of four scientists from El Colegio de la Frontera Sur (ECOSUR), a research center in southeast Mexico, trekked into the burned area. Anna Horváth and Odette Preciado-Benítez are wildlife biologists who specialize in studying bats. Benigno Gómez studies tropical ecology, especially insects, and Darío Navarrete-Gutiérrez is a forest biologist. They were trying to find ways to repair the damage and bring the forest back to life.

But it seemed hopeless, as every tree, bush, flower, and vine that could produce seeds for new growth had been destroyed in the flames. Could the forest ever grow again?

Okay, it's your turn. If you were one of the forest biologists trying to heal the land after the fire, what would you do? Using what you know about the power of scat, can you find a solution to this problem?

BRAINSTORMING SOLUTIONS

Well, to regrow a forest, you need to plant seeds, of course. But it takes tens of thousands of seeds to recreate a forest. You'd need hundreds of people working to plant them, and the burned areas were in remote, mountainous terrain, much of it impossible to reach with a car or truck. It would take a long time and be incredibly expensive.

You need a way to spread seeds quickly over a huge area. Perhaps you could drop seeds from an airplane? Shoot them out of a cannon? If only seeds could fall from the sky like raindrops!

But here's another problem to solve: many of the rainforest plants have seeds, like the chokecherries eaten by bears, that are very hard to germinate. Fewer than 10 percent will germinate when planted by hand. They sprout best after passing through an animal's digestive system.

So the ECOSUR biologists decided that the way to get the forest growing again was to let nature do the work for them. But what kind of animals would make the best gardeners?

FLYING FARMERS

Anna Horváth and Odette Preciado-Benítez are experts on bats, especially the bats of Mexico. They knew that in the tropics, dozens of species of bats drink nectar from flowers or eat fruit instead of insects as most bats in northern climates do. After stuffing themselves with tasty fruits, fruit bats fly long distances back to their daytime sleeping spots. And because no one wants to sleep in a

These bats don't eat bugs—they have a sweet tooth.

poopy mess, they get rid of waste on the way back, before getting to their roosts. The bats defecate in midair, dropping tiny bat bombs—filled with seeds! Bats drop so many seeds as they poop that botanists call it "seed rain."

Other creatures eat fruits and swallow seeds too, especially birds. But in the daytime, forest birds don't like to fly across large open areas. Too dangerous—they might get eaten by a hawk! Birds tend to stay under the canopy of trees and poop while sitting on branches, often on the same perch over and over again. Bats, flying at night, are under cover of darkness and will cross large open areas in search of food.

Bats soar high over
the rainforest.

HOW TO LURE A BAT

But the fire areas were so big and so damaged that there were no food plants left there. The bats had no reason to travel all that distance. So how to lure fruit-eating bats? Well, use fruit!

The scientists went to the farmers market in the nearby town of San Cristóbal and bought pounds of soft, smelly bananas and ripe mangos. The fruit was hung from dead trees and bushes in the center of the burned areas to lure the bats. Fruit bats have a keen sense of smell, and they quickly picked up the scent of the bait. Soon, hundreds of bats were soaring over the destroyed forest every night.

But would the bats bring enough seeds to reseed the forest? In order to find out exactly what each bat was pooping out, the team decided they would have to take a closer look. They set up mist nets, which are very fine-meshed nets strung on poles, sort of like a volleyball net. Occasionally, bats would get tangled in the mesh. The captured bats were then gently untangled and placed in soft cloth bags. More than seven hundred bats of nineteen different species were captured. As soon as each bat had deposited a scat sample in the bag, it was released to soar back into the sky.

Then came the dirty work—the scientists spent hours dissecting each bat poop and figuring out what kinds of seeds were in it. They counted the numbers of seeds transported by each different species of bat.

They were delighted to find that not only was the bat scat packed with seeds, but most of the seeds were from species of trees that are called pioneer plants. These are hardy, fast-growing plants

The rainforest is a rich habitat for countless plants and animals.

Bison poop enriches the prairie and spreads seeds far and wide.

that move into areas where the soil has been burned or disturbed. The pioneers grow quickly and soon provide shade and moisture for other plants to grow. The bats were dropping seeds from pioneer trees like wild fig, wild cherry, potato tree, spiked pepper tree, and wild coffee tree. When the team planted some of the seeds in potting soil, more than 50 percent of them germinated immediately.

Every day, the team placed new bananas and mangos to replace the ones the bats had feasted on. And every night, the bats flew to the fruit, dropping seeds as they flew. In a few weeks, the charred and blackened lands were covered with sturdy green shoots and baby trees. The scientists estimate that the seeds in bat droppings accounted for 95 percent of all new growth. Slowly, drenched in a healing rain of bat scat, the devastated forest was reborn.

Black-backed jackals eat berries and disperse seeds over the savanna.

THE BEGINNING

No matter where you go around the globe, we're beginning to figure out that scat is an essential part of healing our planet. Sleepy koalas are helping the Australian outback recover from wildfires—their poop rains down on the dry land and powers the growth of new trees. In the western parts of North America, bison scat is fertilizing the soil, turning lands that were once a barren dust bowl into green prairie. The rich earth created by the scat of Arctic foxes makes green oases in the tundra landscape. Jackals poop out seeds and nutrients on the savannas of South Africa. Panda poop fertilizes bamboo forests in China, while giraffe scat spreads seeds far and wide over the grasslands of Kenya.

Bat scat, bear scat, bird scat, hippo scat . . . a tiny speck of mouse scat or a huge blast of whale scat. Scat has hidden powers we're only just beginning to discover. The more we hold our noses and unlock the mysteries of scat, the more ways we find it can help us make a better Earth.

A Field Guide to Scat in Your Neighborhood
Written by George Steele

No matter where you live, there are probably more animals around than you think. They often are hard to spot, but scat is a certain clue to their presence. Remember, every living thing has to excrete!

Keep an eye out for scat in unexpected places. For example, you might see the white splats of bird guano in a parking lot or on a sidewalk. Or you might find a few grains of dark brown "rice" in a drawer—could be mice! Maybe you'll come across a big splat of bear scat in a national park. Or you might spy teeny, tiny dots of spider scat underneath a spider web on a porch.

SAFETY MATTERS

Caution! As you investigate the scat in your neighborhood, do not handle it or inhale it. Some wildlife diseases can be spread through touching or even inhaling dust from scat of animals like raccoons.

Take a photo instead of collecting actual specimens.

Instead of collecting scat, take a photo. Put something in the photo to show how big the specimen is.

A small ruler or something like a coin placed near the scat can give a sense of size and help you remember how big the scat was.

INSECTS

Insect poop, often called frass, comes in a wide range of shapes, sizes, and textures. Perhaps you've noticed little dark specks along a window frame. They're flyspecks, the dried-up remains of liquid scat from house flies. Or maybe while combing a dog, you see tiny black dots at the base of its hairs. That's the droppings of fleas.

One of the best ways to locate monarch butterfly caterpillars is to look for tiny, barrel-shaped droppings on the leaves of milkweed. If you spot this scat, look on the underside of the leaves above the scat, and you might find the hiding caterpillar.

Monarch caterpillar scat.

This cormorant is letting it fly!

BIRDS

Bird scat is often very liquid without much shape. For many birds, it looks like a splash of whitewash.

The scat of insect-eating birds like swallows will often contain crushed pieces of the exoskeleton of the insects that they have eaten. Sometimes you can recognize different parts of the insect's body, including leg and body segments and elytra, the hard wing coverings of beetles.

Berry-eating birds like mockingbirds and cardinals carry the seeds of the berries that they've been eating. This scat is best found in late summer into early winter when birds are feasting on the ripe berries. Look for this scat where birds like to perch, including fence posts, playground equipment, and along walk-ways and pavement under overhead wires.

The scat of plant-eating birds is usually quite distinctive. Any place where you see geese congregating on a park lawn or playing field, you'll find their greenish, mushy droppings. Close examination will reveal bits of undigested plant material, mostly grass, that the geese have been grazing on.

MAMMALS

Herbivores (plant eaters) like rabbits and deer often leave small, round pellets of scat. Rabbit scat is dotted here and there in the underbrush.

Deer, moose, and elk deposit their scat in a big pile. If they've been eating dry bark and twigs, the scat is hard pellets. If they've been feasting on apples or lush green grass, it can be just a big, wet pile.

Carnivores (meat eaters) like weasels often have traces of bones in their scat. But many animals that you might think of as meat eaters, like foxes and coyotes, are **omnivores**, meaning they eat all sorts of things. Fox scat, for instance, might have traces of mouse bones and berry seeds in the same dropping.

Wetland animals like otters might have fish scales or crab shells in their scat.

Canada goose scat.

Cottontail rabbit scat.

White-tailed deer pellets.

Deer scat after eating juicy plant material.

Fox scat.

Otter scat.

GLOSSARY

autocoprophagy: when an animal eats its own scat

carnivore: an animal that eats almost nothing but meat

coprolite: a piece of fossilized scat

coprophage: an organism that eats scat

coprophagy: eating scat to obtain extra nutrients

defecate: to rid the body of waste materials

diatom: a one-celled algae with a cell wall made of silica

dung: solid waste from animals, usually referring to large herbivores like horses or bison

ecosystem: a community of living things that interact with each other and with their environment

excrete: to rid the body of waste materials

frass: the scat of insects

germinate: when a seed begins to grow

guano: the scat of flying animals like birds or bats

herbivore: an animal that eats only plants

hormones: chemicals produced by an animal's body that travel through the blood carrying messages to the organs and cells

krill: a small, shrimplike animal that drifts in the open sea

nutrients: minerals, vitamins, and chemicals that are essential to living things

omnivore: an animal that eats both plants and animals

phytoplankton: tiny specks of algae that drift in the sea

scat: the waste material of wild animals

scarify: to make holes, scratches, or openings in a surface

BIBLIOGRAPHY

American Museum of Natural History. "What Fossilized Scat Shows About *T. rex* Bite." June 14, 2019. https://www.amnh.org/explore/news -blogs/on-exhibit-posts/fossilized-scat-t-rex-bite.

Bagla, Pallava. "Tigers Tracked by Their Scat." *Science*. June 17, 2009. https://www.science.org/content/article/tigers-tracked-their-scat.

Dance, Amber. "From tiger scat to DNA to—hopefully—survival." *Knowable Magazine*. September 17, 2019. https://knowablemagazine.org /article/living-world/2019/tiger-scat-dna-conservation.

Eiseman, Charley and Noah Charney. *Tracks & Sign of Insects and Other Invertebrates: A Guide to North American Species*. Mechanicsburg, PA: Stackpole Books, 2010.

Elbroch, Mark and Eleanor Marks. *Bird Tracks & Sign: A Guide to North American Species*. Mechanicsburg, PA: Stackpole Books, 2001.

Greenberg, Joel. *A Feathered River Across the Sky: The Passenger Pigeon's Flight to Extinction*. New York: Bloomsbury, 2014.

Greenfieldboyce, Nell. "The biggest whales can eat the equivalent of 80,000 Big Macs in one day." NPR Science. November 3, 2021. https:// www.npr.org/2021/11/03/1051650199/the-biggest-whales-can-eat -the-equivalent-of-80-000-big-macs-in-one-day.

Halfpenny, James. *Scats and Tracks of North America: A Field Guide to the Signs of Nearly 150 Wildlife Species*. Washington, DC: Rowman and Littlefield, 2008.

Halfpenny, James and Jim Bruchac. *Scats and Tracks of the Northeast: A Field Guide to the Signs of 70 Wildlife Species.* Washington, DC: Rowman and Littlefield, 2001.

Millgate, Kris. "What Happens When You Plant a Pile of Bear Scat?" *Cool Green Science*, The Nature Conservancy. Updated October 3, 2018. https://blog.nature.org/2017/05/10/what-happens-when-you-plant -pile-bear-scat/.

Montoro, Alexander. "Seed dispersal by fruit-eating bats essential to tropical reforestation." *Mongabay.* July 8, 2015. https://news.mongabay .com/2015/07/seed-dispersal-by-fruit-eating-bats-essential-to -tropical-reforestation/.

Paton, Alexandra J., Jessie C. Buettel, and Barry W. Brook. "Evaluating scat surveys as a tool for population and community assessments." *Wildlife Research*, 49(3):206-214 (2021). December 3, 2021. https:// bioone.org/journals/wildlife-research/volume-49/issue-3/WR21056 /Evaluating-scat-surveys-as-a-tool-for-population-and-community /10.1071/WR21056.short.

Pokagon, Simon. "The wild pigeon of North America." *Chautauquan* 22, no. 2 (November 1895). https://archive.org/details/wildpigeonof nort00poka/page/202/mode/2up.

Preciado-Benítez, Odette, Benigno Gómez y Gómez, Darío Navarrete-Gutiérrez, and Anna Horváth. "The Use of Commercial Fruits as Attraction Agents May Increase the Seed Dispersal by Bats to Degraded Areas in Southern Mexico." *Tropical Conservation Science* 8, no. 2 (June 2015): 301–317. https://doi.org/10.1177/194008291500800203.

Romano, Marta C, Alba Zulema Rodas, Ricardo A Valdez, Sandra Elizabeth Hernández, Francisco Galindo, Domingo Canales, and Dulce Maria Brousset. "Stress in Wildlife Species: Noninvasive Monitoring of Glucocorticoids." *Neuroimmunomodulation* 17, no. 3 (February 2010): 209–212, https://doi.org/10.1159/000258726.

Romm, Cari. "How Poop Made the World Go 'Round." *The Atlantic*. November 3, 2015. https://www.theatlantic.com/science/archive/2015/11/how-the-poop-of-giant-animal-species-kept-the-world-healthy/413608/.

Solly, Meilan. "East Africa's Mara River Relies on Hippo Poop to Transport a Key Nutrient." *Smithsonian Magazine*. May 2, 2019. https://www.smithsonianmag.com/smart-news/east-africa-relies-hippo-poop-transport-key-nutrient-180972086/.

Spice, Byron. "Carnegie Mellon Researchers Use Autonomous Air-boats To Monitor Hippo Dung in Kenya's Mara River Basin." Carnegie Mellon University. May 22, 2014. https://www.cmu.edu/news/stories/archives/2014/may/may22_hippowaterquality.html.

Tkaczyk, Filip. *Tracks & Sign of Reptiles & Amphibians: A Guide to North American Species.* Mechanicsburg, PA: Stackpole Books, 2015.

SOURCE NOTES

Chapter 2

P 12. "I was pretty excited when I saw . . ." Trish Stockton in "What Happens When You Plant" https://blog.nature.org/2017/05/10/what -happens-when-you-plant-pile-bear-scat/

P 13. "We've tried to grow these before . . ." Kevin Gaalaas in "What Happens When You Plant" https://blog.nature.org/2017/05/10/what -happens-when-you-plant-pile-bear-scat/

Chapter 3

P 18. "[It's] almost like gold .." Uma Ramakrishnan in "From tiger scat to DNA" https://knowablemagazine.org/article/living-world/2019 /tiger-scat-dna-conservation

Chapter 5

P 40. "That amount of food . . ." Matthew Savoca in "The Biggest Whales" https://www.npr.org/2021/11/03/1051650199/the-biggest-whales-can -eat-the-equivalent-of-80-000-big-macs-in-one-day

Chapter 6

P 46. "I have seen them . . ." Simon Pokagon in "The Wild Pigeon of North America" https://archive.org/details/wildpigeonofnort00poka /page/202/mode/2up

PHOTO CREDITS

ACKNOWLEDGMENTS

Thank you to George Steele, walking encyclopedia of wildlife lore and scat expertise. Thanks especially for writing the "A Field Guide to Scat in Your Neighborhood" in the back matter.

And thank you to the photographers who let me use their images for this book. You give us a new way to look at the beauty of scat!

INDEX

Note: page numbers in *italics* indicate photographs.